LANGUAGE ARTS
EXPLORER JUNIOR

D1520596

Prepositions

over

up

on

across

in

by Katie Marsico

CHERRY
LAKE
Publishing

A note on the text:
Certain words
are highlighted
as examples of
prepositions.

Bold, colorful
words are
vocabulary words
and can be found
in the glossary.

Published in the United States of America by Cherry Lake Publishing
Ann Arbor, Michigan
www.cherrylakepublishing.com

Content Adviser: Lori Helman, PhD, Associate Professor, Department of
Curriculum & Instruction, University of Minnesota, Minneapolis, Minnesota

Photo Credits: Page 9, ©oliveromg/Shutterstock, Inc.; page 12, ©Dmitry
Naumov/Shutterstock, Inc.; page 13, ©NatUlrich/Shutterstock, Inc.;
page 15, ©Africa Studio/Shutterstock, Inc.; pages 16 and 19, ©Monkey
Business Images/Shutterstock, Inc.; page 20, ©Maria Dryfhout/
Shutterstock, Inc.

Library of Congress Cataloging-in-Publication Data
Marsico, Katie, 1980–
  Prepositions / By Katie Marsico.
      pages cm. — (Language Arts Explorer Junior)
  Includes bibliographical references and index.
  ISBN 978-1-62431-182-6 (lib. bdg.) —
ISBN 978-1-62431-248-9 (e-book) — ISBN 978-1-62431-314-1 (pbk.)
  1. English language—Prepositions—Juvenile literature. I. Title.
  PE1335.M36 2013
  428.2—dc23   2013005599

Cherry Lake Publishing would like to acknowledge the work
of The Partnership for 21st Century Skills. Please visit www.p21.org
for more information.

Printed in the United States of America
Corporate Graphics Inc.
July 2013
CLFA13

Table of Contents

CHAPTER ONE

Preparing for a Project

Abby and her friend Nate laid a piece of cardboard on the kitchen table at her house. They had a big job ahead of them. Their teacher had asked them to build a model of their town. The assignment sounded like fun. Yet Abby and Nate also knew it would take careful planning.

"Ready for a little construction work?" asked Abby with a smile. "First, I think we should paint green around the edges of the cardboard."

"It will look just like grass," added Nate.

"We could cut up black construction paper into strips with scissors. Then we can use the strips to add roads," said Abby. "I think the paper is in my basement. I bought clay for the buildings."

"Perfect," replied Nate. "Now let's get going. Remember, we need to finish this model by tomorrow morning!"

at of on by in with for from to

Abby and Nate used **prepositions** when they talked about their project. Prepositions show **relationships** between words. The most common prepositions are *at, by, for, from, in, of, on, to,* and *with.* Prepositions connect a noun or pronoun in a sentence to another word or group of words. This noun or pronoun is called the object of the preposition. Together, the preposition and the object are called a prepositional **phrase**. Abby and Nate cut up the paper *with scissors.* The prepositional phrase also includes any adjectives connected to the object. These could be descriptive words, such as *red, big,* and *smart.* They could also be words that tell how many, such as *some,* or words that indicate which one, such as *a, the,* or *their.* They were building a model *of their town.*

THINK ABOUT IT

Extra Examples

Nate put the lid on the paint bottle.
Preposition: on
Object of the preposition: bottle
Prepositional phrase: on the paint
Connection: The preposition connects the lid to where Nate put it—on the paint.

Abby cleaned the paintbrush with a rag.
Preposition: with
Object of the preposition: rag
Prepositional phrase: with a rag
Connection: The preposition connects the paintbrush to how Abby cleaned it—with a rag.

CHAPTER TWO

A Look at Prepositions

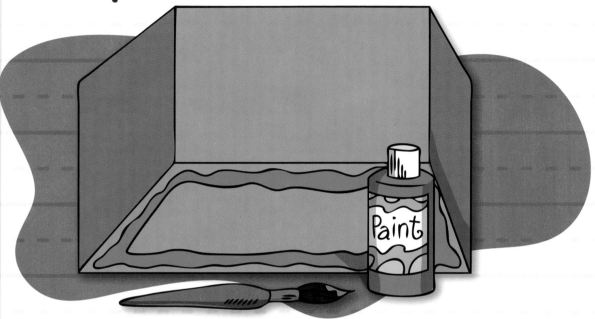

"The paint should dry by the time we finish cutting the construction paper," said Nate. He put his brush in the sink. "We should leave it alone for a little while. Otherwise we will smear the paint."

The prepositions *by* and *for* show relationships that involve time. For example,

Nate used the preposition *for* to connect *a little while*—the amount of time the paint needed to dry. The words *about, after, at, before, from, in, of, on, past,* and *to* are also prepositions that deal with time.

"I will glue 10 strips of black paper across the rest of the cardboard to make the roads," said Abby. "Should we add a piece of blue paper on the right side? I just remembered that a stream runs through the east part of our town."

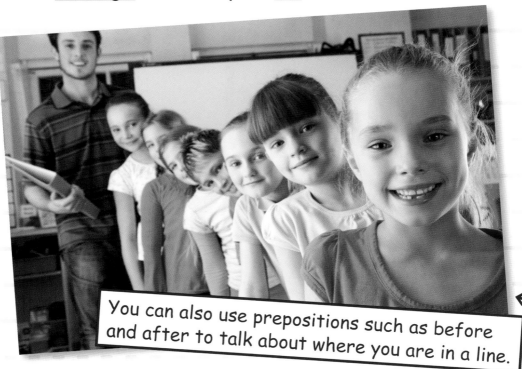

You can also use prepositions such as before and after to talk about where you are in a line.

The prepositions *across*, *of*, *on*, and *through* make connections that involve places and directions. *Around*, *at*, *down*, *from*, *in*, *inside*, *to*, *up*, and *with* also show location.

To get a copy of this activity, visit www.cherrylakepublishing.com/activities.

STOP! DON'T WRITE IN THE BOOK!

ACTIVITY

Locate and List!

Locate and list all the prepositions in the following sentences:

"My mom keeps a pair of scissors in this drawer," said Abby. "Hmm, they're not there. No worries! I will check the craft box under her bed."

"I have scissors and glue inside my backpack," replied Nate. "I keep them with the rest of my school supplies."

"OK," said Abby. "Then I will just make a quick trip to the basement. I think the paper is on the shelf above my dad's desk."

Answers: in, under, inside, with, of, to, on, above

Prepositions help show how Nate and Abby will make their model look like their town.

"The stream is a great idea, Abby!" said Nate. "We want this model to look as much like our town as possible. I will cut the blue paper and cover one side of it with glue." The prepositions *like* and *with* connect words involving how something appears. They also help show the **manner** in which an action is carried out. The terms *by*, *in*, and *on* are used the same way. For example, Nate used *like* to show how he hoped the model would look.

"I am going to start working on the buildings," said Abby. "I bought special clay for our project."

In this case, the preposition *for* connects an action and its **purpose**. It shows the relationship between the project and the reason Abby bought special clay.

"I got modeling clay for $5.00 at the craft store," Abby added. The preposition *for* can also connect words to measurements and amounts.

People use prepositions such as *for* in many situations—including when they visit a store.

"Abby, I see our work *as* a great success," said Nate once they finished everything. The preposition *as* connects words that deal with the state of something, or the way something is. People use *at*, *by*, *for*, *in*, and *on*, the same way. Here, *as* links *success* to the state of Nate and Abby's work.

STOP! DON'T WRITE IN THE BOOK!

To get a copy of this activity, visit www.cherrylakepublishing.com/activities.

ACTIVITY

Read and Rethink

Read the following conversation between Nate and Abby. Then rewrite it, filling in the blanks using prepositions:

"Where did you get the green paint?" asked Nate.
     "I went shopping ____ the hardware store," said Abby. "I bought green paint ____ $6.00."

Why are prepositions important when people talk about activities such as shopping for paint?

CHAPTER THREE

Pay Attention to Punctuation!

Commas, periods, and other punctuation marks help make your ideas clear and easy to understand when you write.

"My mom will help us put our model in her car," said Abby. "Do you want to carry it into the classroom with me tomorrow morning?"

"Sure!" shouted Nate as he headed out her front door. "I will see you at 8:00 in the morning! Let's meet by your locker."

Commas, question marks, exclamation marks, and periods are all examples of **punctuation** that follow prepositional phrases. Punctuation usually comes after the object of the preposition. It rarely comes directly after the preposition itself. Also, most of the time, prepositions do not end sentences.

THINK ABOUT IT

Extra Examples

"With which friend did you work on your project?" asked Abby's sister the next morning. Here, the word *with* sits right beside its object in Abby's sister's question. This is the best place for the preposition. Sometimes, a person speaking might put it at the end of the sentence. Then the sentence would be, "Which friend did you work on your project with?"

"You guys did a super job with this model," their teacher said Monday morning.

"Thanks," replied Abby. "We made it all by ourselves. Nate and I worked on it for three hours on Sunday."

"Yep," added Nate proudly. "We definitely had a great time with this project."

"I see that," said their teacher. "How about we keep the model outside the principal's office? That way, everyone who comes inside the school will be able to see it!"

People rely on prepositions to share ideas.

Prepositions are not just useful when it comes to talking about class projects. Speakers and writers rely on them all the time to show the relationships between words in a sentence. Prepositions are like bridges. They build connections to help people understand!

Think about what prepositions you use the next time you talk to one of your friends or relatives!

ACTIVITY

Read and Rethink!

Read the conversation below. Then rewrite what Nate and Abby say to each other by filling in the blanks with prepositions:

"The principal asked to see us ____ recess!" Nate told Abby.

"Ugh," replied Abby. "I hate when I get called ____ his office."

"Don't worry," said Nate. "I think he wants to meet ____ us ____ a good reason this time. He told me he only needed to talk to us ____ a few minutes."

"I bet the discussion will be ____ our model," Abby said.

"Probably," answered Nate. "He mentioned that he planned to put it ____ his office. It will be the first thing people notice when they walk ____ the stairs."

"Now I am getting excited," said Abby.

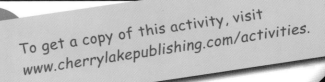

To get a copy of this activity, visit www.cherrylakepublishing.com/activities.

21

Glossary

manner (MAN-ur) the way in which something is done

phrase (FRAYZ) a group of words that have a meaning but do not form a sentence

prepositions (prep-uh-ZISH-uhnz) words that show the relation of a noun or pronoun to other items in a sentence

punctuation (puhngk-choo-AY-shuhn) the use of periods, commas, and other marks to help make the meaning of a sentence clear

purpose (PUR-puhs) the reason or goal for something

relationships (ri-LAY-shuhn-ships) the ways in which two or more things are connected

For More Information

BOOK

Doyle, Sheri. *What Is a Preposition?* North Mankato, MN: Capstone Press, 2013.

WEB SITE

ESL Games Plus—Prepositions Wheel Game
http://www.eslgamesplus.com/preposition-interactive-grammar-game-for-esl-wheel-game/
Try this game to test your knowledge of prepositions.

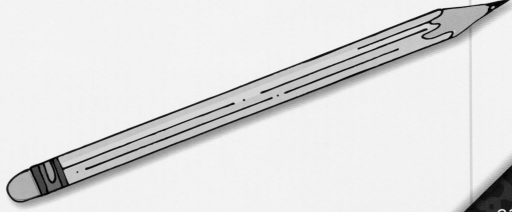

Index

About the Author

Katie Marsico is an author of reference books for children and young adults. She lives outside Chicago, Illinois, with her husband and children.